from SEA TO SHINING SEA
NEW MEXICO

By Judith Bloom Fradin and Dennis Brindell Fradin

CONSULTANT

Robert L. Hillerich, Ph.D., Professor Emeritus, Bowling Green State University;
Consultant, Pinellas County Schools, Florida

CHILDREN'S PRESS
A Division of Grolier Publishing
Sherman Turnpike
Danbury, Connecticut 06816

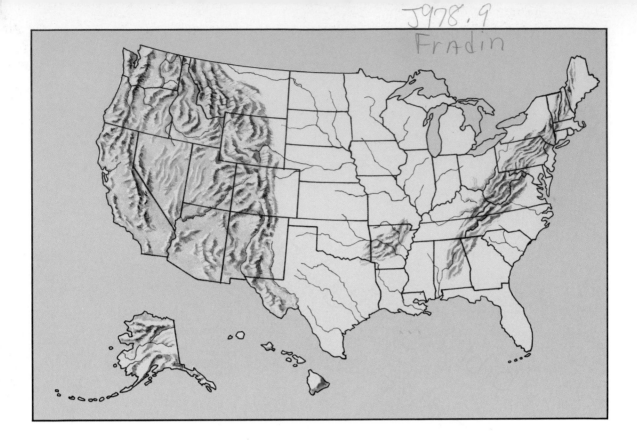

New Mexico is one of the four states in the region called the Southwest. The other states in the Southwest are Arizona, Oklahoma, and Texas.

For Harold Bloom, a wonderful father and father-in-law

For his help, the authors thank Robert Torrez, state historian at the Records Center and Archives in Santa Fe

Front cover picture: Shiprock, on the Navajo Reservation; page 1: Santa Fe Baldy, Sangre de Cristo Mountains; back cover: geologic formations at Tent Rocks, near Cochiti

Project Editor: Joan Downing
Design Director: Karen Kohn
Typesetting: Graphic Connections, Inc.
Engraving: Liberty Photoengraving

Library of Congress Cataloging-in-Publication Data

Fradin, Judith Bloom.
  New Mexico/ by Judith Bloom Fradin and Dennis Brindell Fradin.
    p.   cm. — (From sea to shining sea)
  Includes index.
  Summary: An introduction to the geography, history, people, cities, and famous sites of the large southwestern state known as "The Land of Enchantment."
   ISBN 0-516-03831-1
   1. New Mexico—Juvenile literature. [1. New Mexico.]
I. Fradin, Dennis B. II. Title. III. Series: Fradin, Dennis B. From sea to shining sea.
F796.3.F74   1993   93-799
978.9—dc20   CIP
                                                          AC

Table of Contents

A Pueblo Indian Corn Dance

Introducing New Mexico

New Mexico is a huge state in the southwestern United States. It was named for Mexico by Spanish explorers. Spain governed Mexico at one time.

New Mexicans feel that their state has a special magic. They call it the "Land of Enchantment." First, there is the magic of the scenery. New Mexico has deep caves and red mountains. It also has a desert with snow-white sand. There is also the magic of New Mexico's past. The state has Indian villages that are nearly 1,000 years old. Santa Fe is the oldest capital city in the United States.

Today, New Mexico is a center for scientific work. The state is also a leading miner of natural gas and oil. Large deposits of copper and coal are found there. Huge amounts of pecans, grapes, and lettuce are grown there.

New Mexico is special in other ways. Where did some of the earliest people in the United States live? Where was the first atomic bomb exploded? Where did artist Georgia O'Keeffe live? Where was astronaut Harrison Schmitt born? The answer to these questions is: New Mexico.

*A picture map
of New Mexico*

*Overleaf: Angel Peak
National Recreation
Area*

The Land of Enchantment

THE LAND OF ENCHANTMENT

New Mexico is about 100 times the size of Rhode Island, the smallest state.

The barrel cactus grows in New Mexico's desert areas.

The Land of Enchantment is shaped almost like a square. Some land overflows the square in the northeast and southwest. The state covers about 121,593 square miles. Of the fifty states, only Alaska, Texas, California, and Montana are bigger.

Five states and another country border New Mexico. Colorado is to the north. Utah is to the northwest. Arizona lies to the west. Texas and Mexico form the southern boundary. Oklahoma and Texas are to the east.

The Rocky Mountains run down the middle of northern New Mexico. The Nacimento, Jemez, and Sangre de Cristo mountains are New Mexico's Rockies. The state's highest point is in the Sangre de Cristos. That is Wheeler Peak, at 13,161 feet above sea level. Only six states have taller mountains.

The Great Plains cover the eastern one-third of New Mexico. Most of the state's ranches and farms are there. Northwestern New Mexico has deep canyons and high mesas. Dry places called deserts cover much of southern New Mexico.

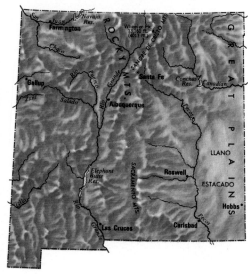

TOPOGRAPHY

| Below Sea Level | 100 m. 328 ft. | 200 m. 656 ft. | 500 m. 1,640 ft. | 1,000 m. 3,281 ft. | 2,000 m. 6,562 ft. | 5,000 m. 16,404 ft. |

CLIMATE

New Mexico is mostly sunny, warm, and dry. The state averages four sunny days for each cloudy one. Summer temperatures often top 90 degrees Fahrenheit. In the desert, the temperature can reach 105 degrees Fahrenheit. New Mexico's winter temperatures often reach 50 degrees Fahrenheit. Yet, winter nights in the mountains can be bone-chilling cold.

Much of New Mexico receives little rain and snow each year. But 300 inches of snow can fall in the mountains. Rainstorms sometimes strike New Mexico. One happened in the spring of 1955. About a foot of rain fell on Lake Maloya in one day.

Left: The Sandia Mountains near Albuquerque

9

RIVERS AND LAKES

The Rio Grande flows down the entire middle of the state. The Pecos River begins near Santa Fe. It flows through New Mexico into Texas. The Gila, Canadian, and San Juan are the state's other major rivers.

Dams have been built on these rivers. They provide water for dry parts of the state. Water is stored in artificial lakes behind the dams. Canals transport the water to cities and farms that need it. The state's largest lake was artificially made. It is called Elephant Butte Reservoir. This lake lies along the Rio Grande.

WOODS AND WILDLIFE

One-fourth of New Mexico is forest. A kind of pine called the piñon is the state tree. Piñon wood burns with a pleasing smell. Piñon nuts have been eaten by New Mexicans for centuries. Firs, oaks, and cottonwoods also grow in New Mexico.

Cactus plants live in the deserts. They can live for long periods with very little water. Yucca plants also grow in the state. The yucca flower is New Mexico's state flower.

Elephant Butte Reservoir

The Land of Enchantment has only a few natural lakes.

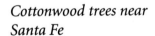

Cottonwood trees near Santa Fe

New Mexico has many kinds of wildlife. The black bear is New Mexico's state animal. Coyotes and prairie dogs live in New Mexico, too. Coyotes are related to dogs and wolves. Prairie dogs make a barking sound. But they are really in the squirrel family. Mountain lions, wild horses, and bobcats are also found in New Mexico.

Wild turkeys, ducks, and woodpeckers can be found in New Mexico. The roadrunner is the state bird. Roadrunners race along roads at 15 miles per hour.

Rattlesnakes live in the desert. These snakes are dangerous. They often make a rattling noise before striking. Tarantulas also live in the desert. They are big, hairy spiders.

Clouds over the Four-Corners area, where the four states of New Mexico, Utah, Arizona, and Colorado touch.

New Mexico has a town named Coyote.

From Ancient Times Until Today

FROM ANCIENT TIMES UNTIL TODAY

Millions of years ago, New Mexico was home to many kinds of dinosaurs. Tyrannosaurus rex lived there. Coelophysis was there, too. This little dinosaur was just 6 feet long. It weighed about 50 pounds. That's about as much as a seven-year-old child weighs.

In 1981, Coelophysis was chosen as New Mexico's state fossil.

In 1979, four New Mexicans made a big discovery. This happened about 60 miles northwest of Albuquerque. There, they found the bones of a huge dinosaur. This creature was 150 feet long. It weighed over 100,000 pounds. It was the longest and one of the largest dinosaurs yet discovered. David Gillette led the uncovering of this dinosaur. He named it Seismosaurus. That means "Earth Shaker."

A dinosaur exhibit at the New Mexico Museum of Natural History

AMERICAN INDIANS

New Mexico was one of the first places American Indians lived. In 1908, George McJunkin, a black cowboy, discovered 10,000-year-old spearheads. He found them near Folsom. They were named Folsom

Opposite page: Chetro Keti Ruin at Chaco National Historical Park

13

points. The Indians who made them belonged to the Folsom Culture.

Then, in 1990, Dr. Richard MacNeish found remains from even earlier people. He found tools at Orogrande Cave. They date back 55,000 years. They are the oldest human relics found in the Americas.

By A.D. 400, Anasazi Indians lived in New Mexico. They grew corn and beans. Anasazi homes were much like apartment buildings. Some had hundreds of rooms.

Because Acoma Pueblo stands atop a high mesa, it is called "Sky City."

The Pueblo Indians are the Anasazis' descendants. The Pueblos include many groups. Among them are the Zuni, Acoma, Hopi, and Taos Indians.

Like the Anasazis, the Pueblo people farmed. They lived in villages called pueblos. Acoma Pueblo is one of the country's oldest towns. It is in western New Mexico. Acoma Indians have lived there for nearly 1,000 years. Acoma Pueblo is called "Sky City." It stands atop a high mesa.

Navajo and Apache Indians lived in New Mexico, too. The Navajos hunted, farmed, and made beautiful blankets. The Apaches were buffalo hunters. They were also great fighters. They tried to protect their land from Spaniards and Americans.

SPANISH EXPLORERS, MISSIONARIES, AND RULERS

A Navajo weaver

Spain conquered Mexico in the early 1500s. The Spaniards hungered for gold. Indians in Mexico told them tall tales. They described a kingdom with golden cities. It was north of Mexico.

A party of Spaniards left Mexico in 1539. They went in search of the golden cities. Heading the party was Marcos de Niza, a priest. A black man named Estevanico came with him. That spring, they explored New Mexico. But they found no golden cities.

Francisco Vásquez de Coronado continued the search (1540-1542). He found no golden cities, either. But he conquered Indian villages in Arizona and New Mexico. Coronado claimed the Southwest for Spain. The Spaniards called the land *Nuevo Mejico*—"New Mexico."

Not until the late 1500s did the Spaniards settle New Mexico. Before they did this, they opened a road in 1581. It linked Mexico with New Mexico. This road followed old Indian trails. Spaniards called it *El Camino Real*—"the Royal Road." It was the first European road in what is now the United States. Today, Interstate 25 south of Santa Fe follows its path.

Oñate carved a message on Inscription Rock in western New Mexico. It can still be read today.

In 1598, Juan de Oñate began Spain's first settlement in New Mexico. He named it San Juan de Los Caballeros. It was New Mexico's first capital. Other Spanish settlements followed. Santa Fe was founded in 1610. It became New Mexico's capital.

Settlers from both Spain and Mexico came to New Mexico. They built *ranchos* (ranches) and farms. The settlers raised cattle and sheep. They grew *frijoles* (beans), wheat, corn, and chili peppers. The Spaniards forced Indians to do much of the work.

Spanish priests also arrived. They wanted the Indians to become Christians. Some Indians did this willingly. Others were forced to become Christians.

The Indians also had to work at the Spanish missions. These were walled villages with a church at the center.

In 1598, Acoma Indians at Sky City rebelled. They killed Juan de Oñate's nephew and other soldiers. Oñate took revenge. In 1599, his men scaled the walls of Sky City. They killed 800 Indians.

Between 1640 and 1680, several Indian uprisings took place in New Mexico. The Indians wanted to worship their own gods. After each uprising, the Spaniards killed or made slaves of the Indian leaders. In 1680, Pueblo leader Popé led a big revolt. The Indians killed 400 Spaniards. Among those killed were 21 priests. Spaniards who survived this uprising left New Mexico.

The ruins of an Indian pueblo and a Spanish mission can be seen at Pecos National Monument.

Diego de Vargas and his men are portrayed at Fiesta de Santa Fe.

The Indians had New Mexico to themselves for twelve years. In 1692, Diego de Vargas recaptured New Mexico for Spain. By 1696, the Spaniards had broken the Pueblo's power. Settlers and priests returned to New Mexico.

In 1706, the Spaniards founded Albuquerque. Ranchers and farmers kept coming from Mexico. By 1820, there were 20,000 settlers in New Mexico.

MEXICAN RULE

Mexico broke free from Spain in 1821. That year, New Mexico came under Mexican rule. New Mexico's settlers were pleased. Americans in the

United States also liked Mexican rule. In 1776, the United States had been founded along the Atlantic Ocean. In 1803, it had gained land west of the Mississippi River. Spanish rulers had kept Americans out of New Mexico. But the Mexican rulers welcomed them.

In 1821, American trader William Becknell opened the Santa Fe Trail. He brought wagons filled with goods from Missouri to Santa Fe. Many more American traders came to New Mexico along the trail. They brought cloth, pans, and tools to Santa Fe. They traded these goods for furs, gold, and silver.

American "mountain men" also came to New Mexico. These men roamed the mountains. They hunted and traded for animal furs. Taos became a gathering place for mountain men. Kit Carson was one of them. This famous trapper and soldier lived in Taos.

During the 1830s, New Mexicans rose up against Mexican rule. They were unhappy about being taxed by Mexico. In 1837, rebels killed New Mexico's governor. They replaced him with José Gonzales. Gonzales was part Indian. But General Manuel Armijo defeated the rebels by 1838. Armijo set up Mexican rule again. He became governor.

Marks made by wagon wheels on what was the Santa Fe Trail can still be seen in New Mexico.

This statue of The Traders *stands at New Mexico State University in Las Cruces.*

The United States Takes Over

By 1845, many Americans felt that the Southwest should be theirs. The United States and Mexico went to war in 1846. General Stephen Kearny took New Mexico for the United States that year.

The United States Congress made New Mexico a territory in 1850. New Mexico then had a territorial governor and a legislature. This moved New Mexico along the road to statehood.

People from eastern and southern states settled in the New Mexico Territory. Some came to ranch. Others came to run stores. Still others searched for gold and silver.

In 1861, the Civil War (1861-1865) began. The northern states fought the southern states in this war. One of the issues was black slavery. Most New Mexicans wanted to stay out of the war. But the war came to them. Southern forces from Texas seized Santa Fe in February 1862. That March, northern troops won the Battle of Glorieta Pass. This was south of Santa Fe. The North gained control of New Mexico. In 1865, the North won the war. All black slaves in the country were freed.

From 1862 to 1864, the North's government forced Indians onto reservations. Thousands of

In 1846, General Stephen Kearny (with paper) proclaimed himself governor of New Mexico. The United States won the Mexican War in 1848.

As of 1861, there were twenty-one black slaves in New Mexico.

Navajos and Apaches were moved to new land. Many died along the way. On the reservations, there was little food and much sickness.

In 1864, the Navajos were allowed to return to northwestern New Mexico. Many Apaches left the reservations. Geronimo was a great Apache warrior. He led the Apaches against settlers and soldiers. In 1886, Geronimo finally surrendered. Fighting ended between Indians and settlers in New Mexico.

Meanwhile, settlers were fighting among themselves. In 1876, cattle ranchers fought for control of Lincoln County. This was called the Lincoln County

Apache warrior Geronimo (seated, third from left) surrendered in 1886.

Billy the Kid's name was William Bonney.

An Atchison, Topeka, and Santa Fe Railroad train at the Glorieta, New Mexico, station in 1880

War (1876-1878). Billy the Kid was a famous outlaw. He killed several law officers during the war. Pat Garrett was sheriff of Lincoln County. He followed the Kid to Fort Sumner, New Mexico, in 1881. There, Garrett shot and killed Billy the Kid.

The railroad first reached New Mexico in 1878. Trains brought more people to New Mexico. By 1910, the territory's population was 327,301. This was enough for statehood. On January 6, 1912, New Mexico became the forty-seventh state.

WARS, OIL, AND DEPRESSION

In 1916, Mexican rebels attacked Columbus, New Mexico. Their leader was Pancho Villa. Sixteen Americans were killed. The United States Army went into Mexico. They tried but failed to catch Villa.

In 1917, the United States entered World War I (1914-1918). New Mexico sent nearly 17,000 soldiers. This was a large number for a state its size.

In 1922, oil was found in New Mexico. Large potash deposits were discovered near Carlsbad. A few years later, the Great Depression (1929-1939)

During the Great Depression, many people who were out of work stood in welfare lines to get meals.

These Navaho Marines were in the South Pacific during World War II.

hit the country. Mines closed. Farmers and ranchers lost their land. New Mexicans suffered through the hard times.

In 1941, the United States entered World War II (1939-1945). About 60,000 New Mexico men and women served their country. Many of them died defending Bataan in the Philippines. Others spent years in Japanese prison camps.

The war's end was helped by a new weapon. The atomic bomb was made in Los Alamos. This town was secretly built just to make the bomb. The first atomic bomb was exploded on July 16, 1945.

This happened at Trinity Site near Alamogordo. In August, two bombs made in Los Alamos were dropped on Japan. They killed 140,000 people. Soon after that, Japan surrendered.

GROWTH AND CHALLENGES

Tourism grew in New Mexico after World War II. Ski resorts opened in the mountains. Motels and restaurants went up in many parts of the state.

In 1950, Navajo Indian Paddy Martinez found uranium in northwest New Mexico. This metal is used in nuclear bombs. Uranium also fuels nuclear power plants. New Mexico became a leading uranium-mining state.

National defense and atomic research are important New Mexico industries. Scientists at Los Alamos National Laboratory study nuclear power. So do scientists at Sandia National Laboratories in Albuquerque. Rockets are tested at White Sands Missile Range.

Nuclear energy creates waste, however. A place near Carlsbad was selected as the country's first nuclear waste dump. Opposition to the project and fears about the environment forced its cancellation in 1993. It would have brought 1,000 new jobs to

The first atomic bomb explosion took place on July 16, 1945.

Nuclear waste comes from nuclear weapons and nuclear power plants.

New Mexico. But, since nuclear waste can be deadly for thousands of years, New Mexicans felt that their safety was more important.

During the 1960s and 1970s, manufacturing increased in New Mexico. The state also enjoyed an oil boom. Thousands of people moved to New Mexico. They found work in its growing industries. The state's population more than doubled between 1950 and 1990. Albuquerque's population quadrupled.

Quadrupled means multiplied by four.

More water was needed for New Mexico's growing population. A big water project was completed in the 1970s. It is the San Juan-Chama Project. It brings water to cities along the Rio Grande.

Water remains a problem in other parts of the state. Aquifers provide most New Mexicans with their water. These are underground areas that hold water. It took millions of years for them to form. New Mexicans use huge amounts of groundwater. Little is being replaced. Some aquifers may run dry. New Mexicans are trying to use less water.

Poverty also worries some New Mexicans. Many of them earn less money than people in nearly every other state. Oil prices dropped during the 1980s. This hurt New Mexico's oil industry. Many

Governor Bruce King

New Mexicans lost their jobs.

In 1991, Bruce King began his third term as governor. In 1993, Gary Johnson was elected to the state's highest office. He and the state legislature are continuing to work to solve New Mexico's problems. For example, New Mexico has started programs to bring more businesses to the state.

New Mexico is also trying to do more business with Mexico. In 1993, a border crossing opened across from Juarez, Mexico. Its purpose is to help New Mexico trade with the country for which it was named.

Overleaf: Teenage girls at the annual Spanish Market in Sante Fe

27

New Mexicans and Their Work

New Mexicans and Their Work

The United States Census counted 1,515,069 New Mexicans in 1990. Only thirteen states have fewer people. New Mexico's population is small. But the state has many different kinds of people.

Three main groups of people have shaped the state. They are the American Indians, the Hispanics, and the Anglos.

Of every 100 New Mexicans, 9 are American Indians (Native Americans).

Of every 100 New Mexicans, 9 are American Indians. This is the highest rate of Indians in the fifty states. Nearly 135,000 Indians live in New Mexico. The Navajos are the largest group. Apaches and several Pueblo groups also live there. Thousands of New Mexico's Indians live on twenty-five reservations. Thousands more live in nineteen pueblos. Others live on farms and in cities.

New Mexico's Indian people have given much to the state. The Zia Sun Symbol came from the Zia Pueblos. It stands for friendship and peace. The Zias used it on their pottery. Today, it is on New Mexico's flag and license plates.

Pueblo Indians still make pottery. Each group has its own design and colors. Navajos weave beau-

About 30,000 black people and nearly 580,000 Hispanics live in New Mexico. Hispanics are people who trace their roots to Spanish-speaking countries.

tiful blankets. Many Indian groups make silver and turquoise jewelry.

New Mexico also has the country's highest percentage of Hispanic people. Almost one in four New Mexicans is Hispanic. This amounts to nearly 580,000 people. Most belong to families that once lived in Mexico and Spain.

Spanish words appear in many place names in New Mexico. For example, *santa* means "holy" or "saint" in Spanish. *Fe* means "faith." So Santa Fe's name means "holy faith." *Rio* is Spanish for "river." *Grande* means "big." The Rio Grande is a large river.

Long ago, the Indians and the Hispanics developed a building style. They called it adobe. Adobe is a sun-dried brick. The bricks are made of clay and straw. Many New Mexico homes and churches are still made of adobe.

White people of non-Hispanic background are called Anglos. Anglos make up the state's largest group of people. Their families came from other states and countries. New Mexico also has a small number of black and Asian people.

NEW MEXICANS AT WORK

About 600,000 New Mexicans have jobs. Almost 145,000 of them work for the government. Many work on New Mexico's government-held lands. These include military bases, national forests, and parklands. Others do scientific work at government laboratories.

More than 3,500 people work at Los Alamos National Laboratory.

About 134,000 of New Mexico's workers sell goods. They include food, computers, clothing, and books. Others sell paintings, photographs, and Indian crafts.

Over 165,000 New Mexicans are service workers. Among them are lawyers and doctors. People who work at resorts and motels are also service workers.

About 42,000 New Mexicans make products. Computer parts and electrical parts are the state's top products. Many foods are made there, too. They include breakfast cereal, salsa (spicy sauce), and chili. Clothing, books, and jet engine parts are also made in New Mexico.

About 20,000 ranchers and farmers work in New Mexico. Cattle are the state's leading farm product. Most are beef cattle, but some are dairy cattle. New Mexico is a leading sheep-raising state.

Red peppers being harvested near Roswell

The state ranks first in the country at growing chili peppers. They go into such foods as chili and ketchup. A popular kind of chili pepper is the New Mexico Big Jim. Hay, cotton, wheat, grapes, pecans, peanuts, and lettuce are also important.

About 15,000 New Mexicans are miners. They help make their state a mining leader. New Mexico is one of the top five natural gas producers. Large amounts of oil and coal also come from New Mexico. The state ranks second to Arizona at mining copper.

An oil-rig worker near Carlsbad

Natural gas is used to heat homes and to cook food.

Overleaf: Taos Pueblo

A Trip Through the Land of Enchantment

A Trip Through the Land of Enchantment

New Mexico offers much to see and do. Visitors enjoy rodeos, skiing, and hot-air ballooning. They also visit Indian villages, resorts, and Spanish towns.

Albuquerque, the State's Largest City

Albuquerque is a good place to start a New Mexico tour. It is not far from the center of the state. Albuquerque lies on the Rio Grande. It was named for the Duke of Alburquerque. He was a Spanish official. The first "r" in his title was dropped from the city's name. Albuquerque has about 400,000 people. No other city in New Mexico is even one-fifth as large.

New and old stand close together in Albuquerque. Sandia National Laboratories is in the city. Scientists there develop new weapons. They take old ones apart. They also work on harnessing the sun's energy.

Albuquerque's Old Town has buildings from 1706. That is when the city was founded. One of these buildings is the Church of San Felipe de Neri.

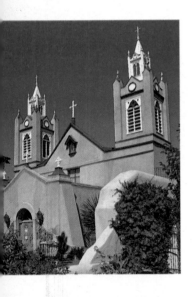

Albuquerque's Church of San Felipe de Neri was built from adobe.

Petroglyph National Monument is even older. Indians made these petroglyphs (rock carvings). They date from 3,000 years ago.

The University of New Mexico (UNM) is in Albuquerque. With almost 25,000 students, UNM is the state's biggest school. Albuquerque is also home to the New Mexico Museum of Natural History. Children enjoy the big, rumbling model of a volcano. They can go inside it to see how a volcano works.

Each fall, Albuquerque hosts the world's largest hot-air balloon rally. This is the International

Left: Albuquerque's Civic Center Plaza
Right: The International Balloon Fiesta

37

Balloon Fiesta. Hundreds of balloons fill the skies above Albuquerque. It is a colorful event.

SANTA FE, THE COUNTRY'S OLDEST CAPITAL

Santa Fe is 6,950 feet above sea level.

Santa Fe is northeast of Albuquerque. This mountain city is the highest of the fifty state capitals. It is better known as the oldest capital in the country.

The Palace of the Governors is the country's oldest public building. It was built in 1610. That is when Santa Fe was founded. The palace was New Mexico's capitol under Spain and Mexico. Later, it was the capitol for the New Mexico Territory. Today, the palace houses the Museum of New

The state capitol, in Santa Fe

Mexico. Displays there cover 450 years of New Mexico history.

Santa Fe also has the country's newest capitol. The new state capitol was completed in 1966. New Mexico's lawmakers meet there today. The building is nicknamed the "Roundhouse." It is shaped like a kiva. That is a round chamber where Pueblo Indians hold ceremonies.

Santa Fe has many art museums. The Museum of Fine Arts displays paintings and sculptures. They were made by people who lived and worked in New Mexico. The Museum of Indian Arts and Culture displays handicrafts. It is known for its Indian pottery, baskets, weaving, and jewelry. The Museum of International Folk Art has more than 125,000 objects. Some of them are toys and dolls from around the world.

Santa Fe is also known for its art galleries and craft shops. Santa Fe's oldest house contains an art gallery. Indians built the house about 800 years ago.

OTHER NORTHERN NEW MEXICO HIGHLIGHTS

Los Alamos National Laboratory is just northwest of Santa Fe. There, scientists created the atomic bomb. Today, they also work on peaceful uses of

The Santa Fe Museum of Fine Arts

Acoma pottery is sold in Gallup.

Children at the Acoma Pueblo

atomic energy. New ways of fighting cancer and AIDS are being developed there. Bradbury Science Museum is part of the laboratory. It shows how atomic energy is used in war and peace.

Just south of Los Alamos is Bandelier National Monument. Its cliff houses have stood for 800 years. Visitors can climb ladders to go into some of them.

West of Bandelier is Chaco Culture National Historical Park. Ruins of a five-story building can be seen there. It is called Pueblo Bonito. Anasazi Indians built it about 1,000 years ago. Pueblo Bonito had about 800 rooms.

Gallup is west of Pueblo Bonita. It is known as the "Indian Capital of the World." The Acoma, Laguna, Zuni, and Navajo reservations are nearby. These Indians sell their goods in Gallup. The Red Rock Museum is near Gallup. It has displays of these Indians' crafts.

The country's biggest Indian reservation is north of Gallup. This Navajo Reservation is also in Arizona and Utah. A famous rock rises above New Mexico's part of the reservation. Non-Indians thought it looked like a ship. They named it Shiprock. But the Navajos call it *Tae-Bidahi*—"Winged Rock." They say that long ago their people were attacked. They hid on the rock. The rock grew wings and flew them to safety.

Just east of the reservation is Farmington. Oil, gas, and coal have helped Farmington grow. It is now the state's fifth-biggest city.

Aztec Ruins National Monument is northeast of Farmington. The Great Kiva can be seen there. It has been restored to look as it did 800 years ago. Anasazis held ceremonies there.

Taos is southeast of Farmington. It is in north-central New Mexico. Many writers and artists live there. Taos has more than 100 art galleries. But it

The Great Kiva at Aztec Ruins National Monument

This picture was taken from the top of Capulin Volcano. The volcano itself is shaped like a 1,000-foot-tall cone.

The Kit Carson home

has only about 4,000 people. Taos is also known for its rich history. The Kit Carson Home and Museum is in Taos. Carson's grave is at nearby Kit Carson State Park.

Taos Pueblo is just outside Taos. This village is over 1,000 years old. The Pueblo Indians believe that they once lived within the earth. Each Pueblo tribe came into the world through a sipapu. That is a hole in the ground. Sipapus are sacred places to the Indians.

Blue Lake is the Taos sipapu. It is near Taos Pueblo. In 1906, the United States government claimed Blue Lake. It became part of a national forest. The Taos people worked to regain their sacred lake. They finally succeeded in 1970. There are many ski areas around Taos. One of them is named Sipapu Ski Area.

Capulin Volcano National Monument is northeast of Taos. It is quiet now. About 10,000 years ago it erupted for the last time. Today, visitors can drive to the top of the volcano. Then they can walk down inside it.

Southeast of Santa Fe is Las Vegas. The Theodore Roosevelt Rough Riders' Memorial and Museum is there. In 1898, the United States and Spain fought a war. The Rough Riders helped the United States win it. Half of its troops were from New Mexico. Roosevelt was their leader.

Tucumcari is southeast of Las Vegas. The town was named for Tocom and Kari. They were a man and woman in an Indian legend. The Tucumcari Historical Museum has an interesting mix of items. They include old saddles, barbed wire, and Folsom spear points.

HIGHLIGHTS OF SOUTHERN NEW MEXICO

Southwest of Tucumcari is Fort Sumner. That is where Pat Garrett killed Billy the Kid. Fort Sumner

Taos Ski Valley

Theodore Roosevelt, who was from New York, later became the twenty-sixth president of the United States.

Billy the Kid's grave

Carlsbad Caverns National Park

Museum has displays about Billy the Kid. The Kid's grave is behind the museum.

South of Fort Sumner is Roswell. In 1930, Robert Goddard came to this southeast New Mexico town. He tested rockets near Roswell. Goddard said that people would one day reach the moon. The Roswell Museum and Art Center has rockets and engines made by Goddard.

Lea County is in New Mexico's southeast corner. It is known for its many rodeo champions. Cowboys and cowgirls ride bucking broncos at rodeos. They also rope calves at these events.

Carlsbad Caverns National Park is south of Roswell. About eighty caves are in the park. The

park was named for the most famous of them, Carlsbad Cavern. Water and minerals carved out these caves. The caves contain strange rock formations. Some of their names are Whale's Mouth, Frozen Waterfalls, and Christmas Tree.

Many science and space studies take place in southern New Mexico. Sunspot is northwest of Carlsbad. It is home to the Sacramento Peak Observatory. The world's largest solar telescope is there. Astronomers use it to study the sun.

West of Sunspot is White Sands National Monument. People slide down the sand dunes

White Sands National Monument

45

Twenty-seven giant satellite dishes on the New Mexico desert make up the VLA.

there. The snow-white sand is made of gypsum. Nearby are an air-force base and missile-testing grounds.

Alamogordo is between White Sands and Sunspot. The International Space Hall of Fame is there. It honors pioneers who studied and explored space.

Northwest of Alamogordo is Socorro. The Very Large Array (VLA) telescope is near Socorro. This is the most powerful radio telescope in the world. It picks up sound waves that are billions of years old.

Truth or Consequences is south of Socorro. In 1950, the town changed its name. The radio show "Truth or Consequences" dared any town to do that. Before 1950, it was called Hot Springs. Elephant Butte Reservoir is near the town. Visitors enjoy swimming, boating, and fishing there.

New Mexico's second-biggest city is south of Truth or Consequences. This is Las Cruces. The name means "the crosses" in Spanish. It was founded in 1848. New Mexico State University started there in 1888. Nearby is the village of Mesilla. It was the South's western capital during the Civil War.

To the northwest is Silver City. Over the years, it has been a gold-, silver-, and copper-mining town. Today, the Phelps Dodge Copper Mines has tours.

There are also "ghost towns" nearby. People left these towns when mining lost importance. Mogollon, once a gold-mining center, was one of those towns. It is northwest of Silver City. Today, artists and carpenters are bringing new life to the town.

The general store at the ghost town of Mogollon

Between Mogollon and Silver City is Gila Cliff Dwellings National Monument. It is a good place to end a New Mexico trip. Indians built homes in these cliffs 700 years ago. The Indians made pictographs on the walls. There are about forty-two rooms in six caves. By climbing a trail, visitors can explore the cliff homes.

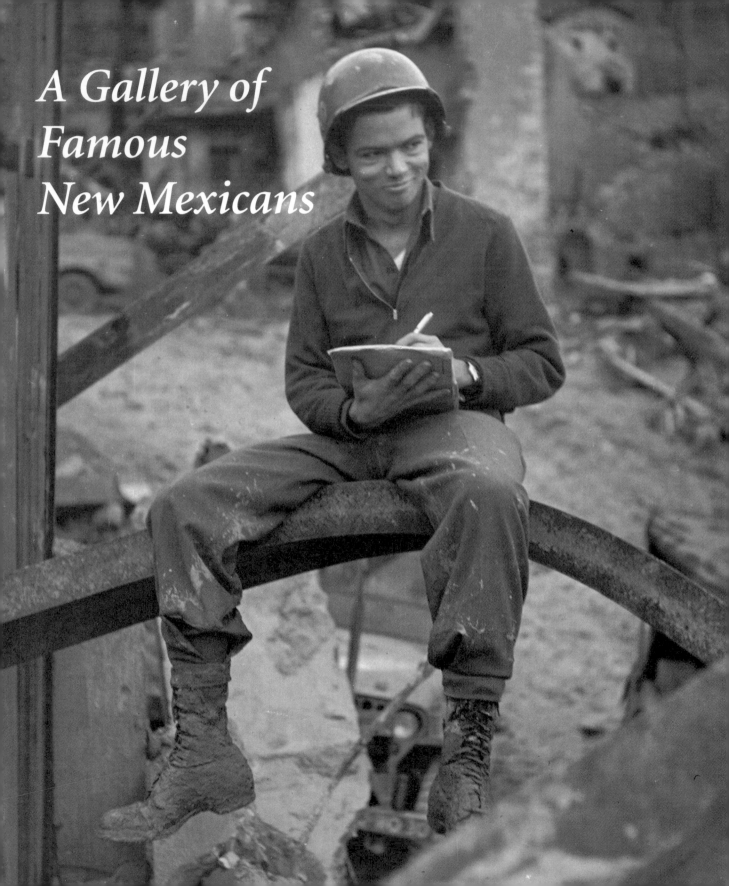

A Gallery of
Famous
New Mexicans

A GALLERY OF FAMOUS NEW MEXICANS

Many New Mexicans have become famous. They include artists, lawmakers, authors, athletes, and even a man who walked on the moon.

Popé (1630?-1692) was born in San Juan Pueblo. That is near Santa Fe. Popé was a Pueblo leader. He wanted to honor the Indian gods. The Spaniards whipped him for doing this. Popé organized the Pueblo Revolt of 1680. The Indians then drove the Spaniards out of New Mexico. Popé then tried to erase all traces of Spanish culture.

Christopher "Kit" Carson (1809-1868) was born in Kentucky. At seventeen, he ran away to Santa Fe. Carson trapped and hunted in the mountains. He married an Indian woman. They had six children. Carson also raised several Indian children. From 1843 to 1868, Carson lived in Taos. Carson helped settle the West. He led northern troops in the Civil War. He also forced thousands of Apaches and Navajos onto reservations (1862-1864). Later, he helped the Navajos return to their own land.

Elfego Baca (1865-1945) was born in Socorro. He became a deputy sheriff in Reserve. There, in

Kit Carson

Opposite page: Bill Mauldin

Maria Martínez

Georgia O'Keeffe

1882, he held off a mob for thirty-three hours. He had arrested a drunken cowboy. The cowboy's friends were angry. A mob shot up the hut where Baca hid. He survived by lying under the hut's mud floor. Baca became a hero. Later, he served as Socorro County's sheriff.

Conrad Hilton (1887-1979) was born in San Antonio, New Mexico. He was elected to New Mexico's first state legislature in 1912. Hilton fought in World War I. In 1919, he began buying and selling hotels. Today, there are more than 400 Hilton hotels worldwide.

San Ildefonso Pueblo was the birthplace of **Maria Montoya Martínez** (1887-1980). Her aunt taught her to make clay pots. Martínez's black-on-black pottery was beautiful. She taught others in her village to make fine pottery, too. This brought money into the poor village. Martínez's pottery is known throughout the world.

Georgia O'Keeffe (1887-1986) was born in Wisconsin. This great artist visited New Mexico in 1929. O'Keeffe so loved the scenery that she moved there. She is remembered for her wonderful paintings of desert scenes.

Dennis Chavez (1888-1962) was born in Los Chavez. He quit school when he was only thirteen.

Chavez had to help support his family. Later, he returned to school and became a lawyer. Chavez served New Mexico in the U.S. House of Representatives (1931-1935) and the Senate (1935-1962). He worked for fair treatment and education of Indians and Hispanics.

"The First Lady of New Mexico Politics" was born in Carlsbad. **Georgia Lee Witt Lusk** (1893-1971) was the daughter and wife of ranchers. Her husband died when she was expecting their third child. Lusk ran a ranch and taught school while raising her sons. Later, she headed New Mexico's schools. Lusk became New Mexico's first congresswoman in 1947. In Congress, she worked for better schools and for war veterans.

Ann Nolan Clark was born in 1898 in Las Vegas, New Mexico. She taught at Indian schools. Her one-room pueblo school could not afford books. Clark began writing her own stories. She wrote children's books about Indians and animals. One book was *Secret of the Andes*. It won the 1953 Newbery Medal.

Pablita Velarde was born at Santa Clara Pueblo in 1918. As a child, Velarde studied ancient Indian rock drawings. She became an artist. Velarde made the Buffalo and Deer Dance mural. It decorates a

Georgia Lusk

In 1988, Velarde was declared a New Mexico "Living Treasure."

"Yer lucky. Yer learnin' a trade."

A Bill Mauldin "Willie and Joe" cartoon

Al Unser, Jr., is on the right in this picture.

wall of the Pueblo Cultural Center in Albuquerque. Velarde also wrote and drew pictures for a book of Indian legends. It is called *Old Father Story Teller*.

Bill Mauldin was born in Mountain Park in 1921. He was a sickly child. He stayed in bed drawing. At eighteen, he joined the army. During World War II, Mauldin drew cartoons for *Stars and Stripes*. That is the army's newspaper. He created Willie and Joe. They were soldiers who expressed what many real soldiers felt. After the war, his cartoons appeared in St. Louis and Chicago newspapers. Mauldin won the Pulitzer Prize in 1945 and 1959.

Harrison Schmitt was born in Santa Rita in 1935. He became a geologist and an astronaut. In 1972, Schmitt spent more than three days on the moon. He was part of the *Apollo 17* flight. He also served as a U.S. senator from New Mexico (1977-1983).

Unser is a great name in auto racing. **Bobby** (born in 1934) and **Al** (born in 1939) **Unser** are both from Albuquerque. Al won the Indianapolis 500 four times. Bobby won it three times. In 1992 and 1994, **Al Unser, Jr.,** won the "Indy." Albuquerque's Unser Boulevard is named for this family of racers.

Nancy Lopez was born in California in 1957. She grew up in Roswell, New Mexico. Lopez won

her first golf tournament when she was nine. At
twelve, she won the New Mexico Women's Amateur
Golf Tournament. Later, she became a great pro
golf champion.

Nancy Lopez

    Birthplace of Harrison Schmitt, Maria Montoya
Martínez, Ann Nolan Clark, and Dennis Chavez . . .

    Home to Georgia O'Keeffe, Robert Goddard,
Nancy Lopez, and Kit Carson . . .

    A land with beautiful scenery and ancient
Indian villages . . .

    A leader in producing natural gas, copper,
pecans, and chili peppers . . .

    This is New Mexico—the Land of Enchantment!

Did You Know?

A flood hit Folsom in 1908. Sarah Rooke, a sixty-eight-year-old telephone operator, called people and warned them to flee. She herself was swept away by the rising water and drowned. By staying at her post, this New Mexico heroine saved many lives.

New Mexican Navajo Indians helped in an unusual way during World War II. The United States had to send messages in secret code. Navajo "code talkers" sent the messages in their language. The Navajo language is so unusual that the enemy could not break the code.

Three New Mexicans were the first people to cross the Atlantic Ocean in a balloon. Ben Abruzzo, Maxie Anderson, and Larry Newman made the crossing in the *Double Eagle II* in 1978.

Smokey Bear State Park at Capitan in southern New Mexico was named for the famous bear. After surviving a 1950 New Mexico forest fire, Smokey was sent to Washington, D.C. There, he lived at the National Zoo. So many children sent Smokey letters at the zoo that he was given his own zip code: 20252.

Elizabeth Garrett, who wrote the state song, "O, Fair New Mexico," was blind. She was the daughter of Pat Garrett, the sheriff who killed Billy the Kid.

Composer Aaron Copland wrote a ballet called *Billy the Kid.*

Two famous New Mexico rock formations look like animals. Camel Rock is north of Santa Fe. Elephant Butte (for which the state's largest lake is named) is near Truth or Consequences.

New Mexico has towns and villages named Pie Town, Mule Creek, House, Rodeo, Sunspot, and Weed. Pie Town was named in honor of a gas station owner who baked tasty pies.

Albuquerque is the highest of the country's fifty biggest cities. It is 6,120 feet above sea level at the highest point.

June Rutherford of Hatch grew the country's biggest pepper in 1975. It was 13.5 inches long.

Lovington, in southeast New Mexico, hosts the World's Greatest Lizard Race each July 4. Hundreds of people watch as children race their pet lizards.

What may be the country's oldest apple orchard is at the town of Manzano. *Manzano* means "apple tree" in Spanish. The orchard is said to date from the mid-1600s.

New Mexico's Indians have interesting foods. The Navajo make corn chowder and acorn bread. The Zunis have an old recipe for jackrabbit stew. Piñon soup is another Indian favorite. It uses nuts from the state tree.

New Mexico Information

State flag

Roadrunner

Piñon tree

Area: 121,593 square miles (the fifth-biggest state)

Greatest Distance North to South: 391 miles

Greatest Distance East to West: 353 miles

Borders: Colorado to the north; Oklahoma and Texas to the east; Texas and the country of Mexico to the south; Arizona to the west; Utah to the northwest

Highest Point: Wheeler Peak in northern New Mexico, 13,161 feet above sea level

Lowest Point: 2,817 feet above sea level, at Red Bluff Reservoir in southeast New Mexico

Hottest Recorded Temperature: 116° F. (at Artesia, on June 29, 1918, and at Orogrande, on July 14, 1934)

Coldest Recorded Temperature: -50° F. (at Gavilan, on February 1, 1951)

Statehood: The forty-seventh state, on January 6, 1912

Origin of Name: New Mexico was named for the country of Mexico

Capital: Santa Fe (the oldest capital in the United States)

Counties: 33

United States Representatives: 3 (as of 1992)

State Senators: 42

State Representatives: 70

State Songs: "O, Fair New Mexico," by Elizabeth Garrett, is the English-language state song; the Spanish-language state song is "Así Es Nuevo Méjico," by Amadeo Lucero

State Motto: *Crescit Eundo* (Latin, meaning "It Grows as It Goes")

Nickname: "Land of Enchantment"

State Seal: Adopted in 1912

State Flag: Adopted in 1925

State Flower: Yucca flower

State Bird: Roadrunner

State Tree: Piñon

State Animal: Black bear

State Gem: Turquoise

State Fossil: Coelophysis

State Insect: Tarantula hawk wasp

State Fish: New Mexico cutthroat trout

State Vegetables: Chili pepper and pinto bean

State Cookie: Biscochito

Some Rivers: Rio Grande, Pecos, Gila, Canadian, San Juan

Some Mountain Ranges: Sangre de Cristo, San Juan, Zuni, Mogollon, San Andres, Sacramento

Some Lakes: Elephant Butte Reservoir, Navajo Reservoir, Conchas Reservoir, Lake Sumner, Bottomless Lakes

Wildlife: Black bears, coyotes, prairie dogs, mountain lions, bobcats, deer, foxes, elk, wild horses, jackrabbits, bighorn sheep, roadrunners, ducks, cranes, hummingbirds, woodpeckers, wild turkeys, many other kinds of birds, rattlesnakes, tarantulas, lizards

Manufactured Products: Computer parts and other electrical equipment, breakfast cereal, chili, other foods, clothing, lumber and wood products, chemicals, concrete, many kinds of metal machinery, buses, parts for jet engines, jewelry

Farm Products: Beef and dairy cattle, sheep, peanuts, pecans, lettuce, grapes, chili peppers, sorghum, wheat, cotton

Mining Products: Natural gas, oil, coal, copper, uranium, gold, silver, molybdenum

Population: 1,515,069, thirty-seventh among the states (1990 U.S. Census Bureau figures)

Major Cities (1990 Census):

Albuquerque	384,736	Rio Rancho	32,505
Las Cruces	62,126	Clovis	30,954
Santa Fe	55,859	Hobbs	29,115
Roswell	44,654	Alamogordo	27,596
Farmington	33,997	Carlsbad	24,952

Yucca flower

Chili peppers

Turquoise

NEW MEXICO HISTORY

A kiva mural at the Kuaua Pueblo

53,000 B.C.—People are living in Orogrande Cave

8,000 B.C.—People from the Folsom Culture are living in New Mexico

A.D. 400—Anasazi Indians are in New Mexico

1100s—Acoma Pueblo, "Sky City," is begun

1500—Navajo and Apache Indians come to New Mexico

1539—Father Marcos de Niza explores New Mexico for Spain

1540—Francisco Vásquez de Coronado explores New Mexico and claims the Southwest for Spain

1581—*El Camino Real* is built

1598—Juan de Oñate founds San Juan de Los Caballeros, the first Spanish settlement and capital in New Mexico

1599—Oñate's men slaughter 800 Indians at "Sky City"

1610—Santa Fe is founded as New Mexico's capital

1680—Popé leads the Pueblo Revolt; 400 Spaniards including 21 priests are killed; other Spaniards flee New Mexico

1692—Diego de Vargas recaptures New Mexico for Spain

1706—Spaniards found Albuquerque

1776—The United States of America is founded

1821—Mexico breaks free of Spain and takes control of New Mexico; William Becknell opens the Santa Fe Trail

1834—New Mexico's first newspaper, *El Crepúsculo de la Libertad (The Dawn of Liberty)* is published at Santa Fe

1846-48—The United States and Mexico fight the Mexican War; Stephen Kearny captures Santa Fe and wins New Mexico for the United States; the United States wins the war and gains New Mexico and other Mexican land in the Southwest

1850—The United States government creates the New Mexico Territory

1862—Southern forces seize Santa Fe during the Civil War; northern forces win the Battle of Glorieta Pass, keeping New Mexico in the Union

1862-64—Apaches and Navajos are forced off their lands and onto reservations

1876-78—Cattlemen fight the "Lincoln County War"

1878—The Atchison, Topeka, and Santa Fe Railroad enters New Mexico

1886—Geronimo surrenders, ending fighting between Indians and settlers in New Mexico

1912—On January 6, New Mexico becomes the forty-seventh state

1917-18—Nearly 17,000 New Mexicans serve after the United States enters World War I

1922—Oil is discovered in New Mexico

1929-39—During the Great Depression, mining and other industries suffer

1941-45—After the United States enters World War II, about 60,000 New Mexico men and women serve; the first atomic bomb is exploded on July 16 near Alamogordo

1950—Paddy Martinez, a Navajo, finds uranium in New Mexico

1966—The state capitol is completed in Santa Fe

1970s—San Juan-Chama Project is completed, bringing water to Albuquerque and other places along the Rio Grande

1972—New Mexico-native Harrison Schmitt explores the moon

1980—Very Large Array (VLA), a powerful radio telescope, is completed near Socorro

1990—The Land of Enchantment's population reaches 1,521,779

1993—A border crossing opens in New Mexico across from Juarez, Mexico

1995—Gary Johnson begins serving his first term as governor

Abandoned wagons can be seen at Fort Union, on the Santa Fe Trail.

MAP KEY

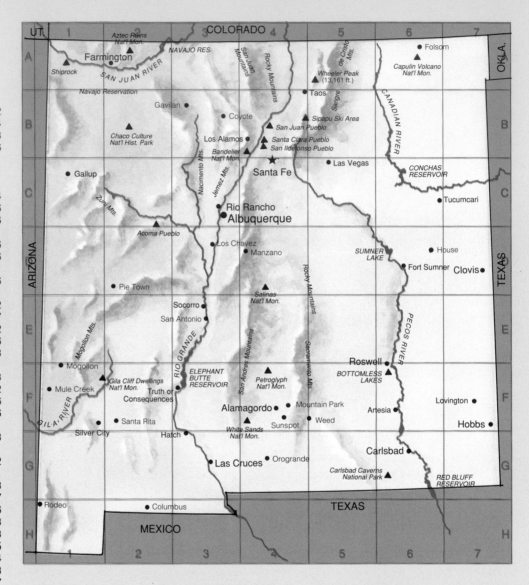

GLOSSARY

adobe: A sun-dried brick made of clay and straw

ancient: Relating to a time early in history

aquifer: A natural underground area that holds water

artificial: Made by people; not occurring naturally

astronaut: A person who is highly trained for spaceflight

astronomer: A person who studies the stars, planets, and other heavenly bodies

billion: A thousand million (1,000,000,000)

butte: A steep mountain or hill that rises sharply above the nearby land

canal: A ditch or other artificial structure through which water flows

canyon: A deep, steep-sided valley

capital: A city that is the seat of government

capitol: The building in which the government meets

climate: The typical weather of a region

enchantment: A quality involving a special beauty, charm, or magic

explorer: A person who visits and studies unknown lands

fossil: The remains of an animal or plant that lived long ago

geologist: A scientist who is an expert on rocks and other structures in the earth

kiva: A round chamber where Pueblo Indians hold ceremonies

legislature: The lawmaking body

manufacturing: The making of products

mesa: A flat-topped mountain or hill

million: A thousand thousand (1,000,000)

mission: A settlement that developed around a church

petroglyph: Carving in a rock

piñon: A kind of pine that is the New Mexico state tree

plain: Nearly level or rolling treeless land

population: The number of people in a place

poverty: A lack of money

pueblo: The kind of building or village that Pueblo Indians live in

radio telescope: The instrument astronomers use to collect radio waves from space

reservation: Land in the United States that is set aside for American Indians

reservoir: An artificially made lake where water is stored

rodeo: A contest in which cowboys and cowgirls ride horses and rope cattle

solar telescope: A telescope used to study the sun

territory: Land that is owned by a country and that has its own government

tourism: The business of providing such services as food and lodging for travelers

volcano: A mountain from which hot rock and other materials erupt

PICTURE ACKNOWLEDGMENTS

Front cover, © **Tom Till;** 1, © Buddy Mays/**Travel Stock;** 2, **Tom Dunnington;** 3, © **Photri, Inc.;** 5, **Tom Dunnington;** 6-7, © Tom Algire/**Tom Stack & Associates;** 8, © Stan Osolinski/**Dembinsky Photo Associates;** 9 (left), © Buddy Mays/**Travel Stock;** 9 (right), **courtesy of Hammond, Incorporated, Maplewood, New Jersey;** 10 (both pictures), © Buddy Mays/**Travel Stock;** 11, © Buddy Mays/Travel Stock; 12, © G. Martin/SuperStock; 13, © Bob Skelly; 14, © Tom Till; 15, © Reinhard Brucker; 17, © Buddy Mays/**Travel Stock;** 18, © Ernesto Burciaga/**Photri, Inc.;** 19, © Bruce Leighty/ mga/**Photri;** 20, Stock Montage, Inc.; 21, **Arizona Historical Society/Tucson #977;** 22, photo by Ben Wittick/ **courtesy Museum of New Mexico #15780;** 23, Stock Montage, Inc.; 24, from *Here Come the Navajo,* Underhill/State Records Center & Archives, Santa Fe; 25, **courtesy Museum of New Mexico #71128;** 27, AP/Wide World Photos; 28, © Jim Richardson/**H. Armstrong Roberts;** 29 (top), © Alison Forbes/**N E Stock Photo;** 29 (bottom), © Larry Allan/ **Photri, Inc.;** 30 (left), © Buddy Mays/**Travel Stock;** 30 (right), © Pam Sharp/**N E Stock Photo;** 31, © Walter Frerck/ **Odyssey Productions;** 32, © George Hunter/**H. Armstrong Roberts;** 33, © Buddy Mays/**Travel Stock;** 34-35, © R. Kord/**H. Armstrong Roberts;** 36, © S. Vidler/**SuperStock;** 37 (left), © Scott Berner/**Photri, Inc.;** 37 (right), © S. Vidler/ **SuperStock;** 38, © Dave Brown/**Tom Stack & Associates;** 39, © Robert Frerck/**Odyssey Productions;** 40 (top), © L.E. Schaefer/**Root Resources;** 40 (bottom), © **Bob Skelly;** 41, © **Tom Till;** 42 (top), © David L. Brown/**Tom Stack & Associates;** 42 (bottom), © **Reinhard Brucker;** 43, © Jackie Linder/**N E Stock Photo;** 44 (top), © **Reinhard Brucker;** 44 (bottom left), © **Gene Ahrens;** 44 (bottom right), © **Jerry Hennen;** 45, © E. Manewal/**SuperStock;** 46, © **Tom Till;** 47, © **Tom Till;** 48, © **John Phillips;** 49, McNitt col. photo #6477, State Records Center & Archives, Santa Fe; 50 (top), **AP/Wide World Photos;** 50 (bottom), UPI/Bettmann; 51, AP/Wide World Photos; 52 (top), **reprinted with permission from the** *Chicago Sun-Times* © 1993; 52 (bottom), AP Photo Color; 53, Wide World Photos, Inc.; 54 (bottom), **U.S.D.A. Forest Service;** 54-55, AP/Wide World Photos; 55, **courtesy of the** *Lovington Daily Leader;* 56 (top), **courtesy Flag Research Center, Winchester, Massachusetts 01890;** 56 (middle), © H. Armstrong Roberts; 56 (bottom), © Buddy Mays/**Travel Stock;** 57 (top), © D. Muench/**H. Armstrong Roberts;** 57 (middle), © Brian Parker/**Tom Stack & Associates;** 57 (bottom), © KEYCOLOR/ZEFA/**H. Armstrong Roberts;** 58, © **North Wind Pictures;** 59, © **North Wind Pictures;** 60, **Tom Dunnington;** back cover, © Buddy Mays/**Travel Stock**

INDEX

Page numbers in boldface type indicate illustrations.

ABOUT THE AUTHORS

From Sea to Shining Sea: New Mexico is the second book Dennis and Judith Fradin have written together. The Fradins both graduated from Northwestern University in 1967. Dennis has been a professional writer for twenty years, and has published 150 books. His works for Childrens Press include the Young People's Stories of Our States series, the Disaster! series, and the Thirteen Colonies series. Judith earned her M.A. in literature from Northwestern University and taught high school and college English for many years. The Fradins, who are the parents of Anthony, Diana, and Michael, live in Evanston, Illinois.